SPORTS SUPERSTARS

T. J. WATT

T0020385

BY ELLIOTT SMITH

WWW.APEXEDITIONS.COM

Copyright © 2024 by Apex Editions, Mendota Heights, MN 55120. All rights reserved. No part of this book may be reproduced or utilized in any form or by any means without written permission from the publisher.

Apex is distributed by North Star Editions:
sales@northstareditions.com | 888-417-0195

Produced for Apex by Red Line Editorial.

Photographs ©: Evan Vucci/File/AP Images, cover, 1, 27; Nick Wass/AP Images, 4–5, 8; Michael Owens/AP Images, 6–7; Shutterstock Images, 10–11, 13, 16–17, 19, 29; iStockphoto, 12; Dan Sanger/Icon Sportswire/AP Images, 14–15; Aaron M. Sprecher/AP Images, 18; Terrance Williams/AP Images, 21; Keith Srakocic/AP Images, 22–23; Don Wright/AP Images, 24–25

Library of Congress Control Number: 2022922644

ISBN
978-1-63738-562-3 (hardcover)
978-1-63738-616-3 (paperback)
978-1-63738-720-7 (ebook pdf)
978-1-63738-670-5 (hosted ebook)

Printed in the United States of America
Mankato, MN
082023

NOTE TO PARENTS AND EDUCATORS

Apex books are designed to build literacy skills in striving readers. Exciting, high-interest content attracts and holds readers' attention. The text is carefully leveled to allow students to achieve success quickly. Additional features, such as bolded glossary words for difficult terms, help build comprehension.

TABLE OF CONTENTS

CHAPTER 1

The Baltimore Ravens are about to score. But T. J. Watt plans to stop them. He lines up with the Pittsburgh Steelers.

T. J. Watt and the Pittsburgh Steelers played the Baltimore Ravens on January 9, 2022.

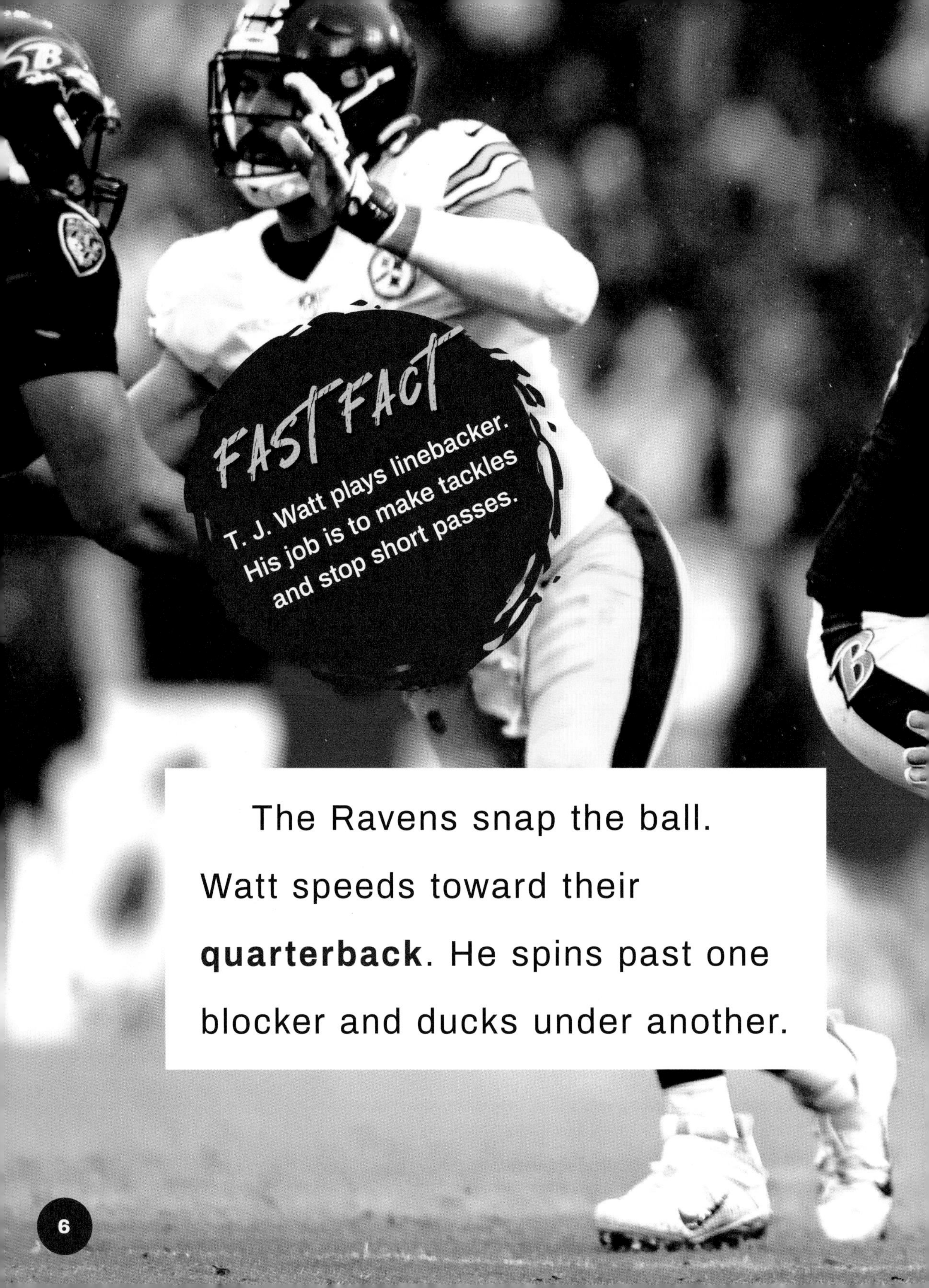

FAST FACT

T. J. Watt plays linebacker. His job is to make tackles and stop short passes.

The Ravens snap the ball. Watt speeds toward their **quarterback**. He spins past one blocker and ducks under another.

Watt (90) pushes past a Ravens blocker.

90
2

Watt reaches the quarterback and tackles him. It's a sack! The Steelers raise their arms and cheer. Soon they have more to celebrate. Watt's **defense** helps them win the game.

A sack happens when a defender tackles the quarterback behind the **line of scrimmage**. Watt's sack tied an NFL record. He had 22.5 sacks during the 2021 season.

◀ Watt had a total of five tackles during the game against the Ravens.

CHAPTER 2

EARLY LIFE

As a kid, T. J. Watt lived in Wisconsin. His family loved football. T. J. played four different positions for his high school football team.

T. J. Watt grew up near Milwaukee, Wisconsin

Wisconsin's football team plays at Camp Randall Stadium in Madison, Wisconsin.

After high school, T. J. went to the University of Wisconsin. He wanted to play **tight end**. But he hurt his knees. At first, he couldn't play. Then he worked hard and got better.

FOOTBALL FAMILY

T. J. has two older brothers, J. J. and Derek. They also played football at the University of Wisconsin. T. J. and Derek later became teammates on the Steelers.

T. J.'s oldest brother, J. J., began playing with the Houston Texans in 2011.

Watt tackles the quarterback of the University of Minnesota football team.

After two years in college, Watt switched to linebacker. Now he could use his strength and speed on defense.

CHAPTER 3

NFL READY

In 2017, Watt decided he was ready for the NFL. He entered the **draft**. The Steelers chose him in the first round.

Players practice and train to get ready for the

Watt became a key part of the Steelers' defense during his first season.

Watt joined the Steelers' defense. He fit right in. He had two sacks and an **interception** in his first NFL game.

STEEL CURTAIN

Pittsburgh has a history of great defense. In the 1970s, its defenders were known as the Steel Curtain. Many people think they were the best defense ever.

The Steelers won the Super Bowl four times in six years from 1975 to 1980.

Watt proved to be a good player. He was smart and athletic. He could spin and push past blockers. He made many tackles.

Watt celebrates after a big play against the Ravens.

90
66

CHAPTER 4

By 2019, Watt was one of the NFL's best pass rushers. He led the NFL in sacks in 2020 and 2021. The Steelers made the **playoffs** in three of his first five seasons.

Watt had at least two sacks in six different games during the 2021 season.

Watt was hard to stop. He could jump high to knock down passes. And he could hit the quarterback's arm to cause fumbles.

BALL HOG

Watt always had an eye on the ball. He forced 22 fumbles in his first five seasons. He also had four interceptions during that time.

A fumble happens when a player drops the ball.

Watt signed a new **contract** in 2021. He became the NFL's highest-paid defensive player. Fans looked forward to more great plays.

Watt signed a $112 million contract in 2021. He agreed to stay with the Steelers for four more years.

COMPREHENSION QUESTIONS

Write your answers on a separate piece of paper.

1. Write a few sentences that explain the main ideas of Chapter 2.

2. Do you prefer to play offense or defense? Why?

3. What position does Watt play in the NFL?

- **A.** linebacker
- **B.** quarterback
- **C.** tight end

4. How could hitting the quarterback's arm cause a fumble?

- **A.** The quarterback couldn't see his teammates.
- **B.** The quarterback could forget the next play.
- **C.** The quarterback could lose his grip on the ball.

5. What does **athletic** mean in this book?

*He was smart and **athletic**. He could spin and push past blockers.*

- **A.** able to read quickly
- **B.** able to move with strength and speed
- **C.** able to dance to music

6. What does **celebrate** mean in this book?

*The Steelers raise their arms and cheer. Soon they have more to **celebrate**.*

- **A.** feel very sad about something
- **B.** feel happy about something
- **C.** give something away

Answer key on page 32.

GLOSSARY

contract

An agreement to pay someone money, often for doing work.

defense

The players who try to stop the other team from scoring.

draft

A system where professional teams choose new players.

interception

A play that happens when a defensive player catches a pass thrown by the other team.

line of scrimmage

The imaginary line separating teams at the beginning of a play.

playoffs

A set of games played after the regular season to decide which team will be the champion.

quarterback

A player who directs the offense and throws the ball.

tight end

A player who is good at blocking and catching passes.

BOOKS

Coleman, Ted. *Pittsburgh Steelers All-Time Greats.* Mendota Heights, MN: Press Box Books, 2022.

Meier, William. *Inside the NFL: Pittsburgh Steelers*. Minneapolis: Abdo Publishing, 2020.

Mitchell, Bo. *The Super Bowl*. Mendota Heights, MN: Apex Editions, 2023.

ONLINE RESOURCES

Visit **www.apexeditions.com** to find links and resources related to this title.

ABOUT THE AUTHOR

Elliott Smith lives in Falls Church, Virginia. He enjoys watching movies, reading, and playing sports with his two children. He has a large collection of Pittsburgh Steelers memorabilia.

ANSWER KEY:
1. Answers will vary; 2. Answers will vary; 3. A; 4. C; 5. B; 6. B